THE LITTLE BOOK OF SCONES

Liam D'Arcy & Grace Hall

All Scone

⬛ SQUARE PEG

Published by Square Peg 2013

2 4 6 8 10 9 7 5 3 1

The Random House Group Limited Reg. No. 954009
Addresses for companies within The Random House Group Limited can be found at:
www.randomhouse.co.uk

A CIP catalogue record for this book is available from the British Library

ISBN 978 0 22 409604 1

The Random House Group Limited supports the Forest Stewardship Council (FSC®), the leading international forest certification organisation. Our books carrying the FSC® label are printed on FSC®-certified paper. FSC® is the only forest certification scheme endorsed by the leading environmental organisations, including Greenpeace. Our paper procurement policy can be found at www.randomhouse.co.uk/environment

Design: Friederike Huber
Illustration: Becka Griffiths
Recipe testing: Emma Marsden
Copy editor: Imogen Fortes

Printed and bound in Great Britain by Clays Ltd, St Ives PLC

For Lacey

CONTENTS

HOW IT ALL BEGAN

We could call it All' Scone ...

The idea to start up a weekend business came to us one sunny afternoon shortly after we first moved to London. We were wandering through Hackney Homemade, a new market set up specifically for street-food sellers starting up in the business. Drooling over the delicious offerings, it seemed a perfect idea to start up a stall at the weekends while we weren't doing our full-time jobs. We'd earn some extra cheese and, even more appealingly, build something from scratch as a couple, with just an idea to get us started.

But what would we sell? Well, that was easy.

We first became friends as children, but lost touch as we grew up, finally finding each other again 10 years later. Soon began a mutual passionate affair with afternoon tea. Dates to country manor houses were commonplace, and when we were not off on such adventures we would bake our own sweet treats, inspired by the delicious things we had scoffed from professional kitchens. Most of the time we ended up making cherry and almond scones, a recipe we had devised ourselves inspired by Grace's lifelong love of cherry bakewells. We cut them into hearts because we were in love and, hey, didn't we know it. Our cherry and almond delights quickly became famous among family and friends and so, when we were deciding what to sell, it was a no-brainer. The name All'Scone, initially a joke, stuck and we haven't looked back since.

Our time as market traders has been invaluable. Every street-food seller makes their product their own, an observation that we made and ran with. We wanted to put scones on the street-food map; we wanted to rebrand them. It was time to take the scone out of the stuffy tearoom and on to the uber-hip streets of East London. We realised that, like the humble cupcake, the scone can carry a vast range of sweet flavours, while also scratching that itch for a comforting sweet treat. We also realised that not many people have discovered this potential, and so we decided to make it our mission to show everyone how much scones can give cakes a run for their money.

Along the way we have learned to have fun with our scones, and we hope this shines through in our recipes. Our flavours have been borne out of our own ideas and favourites, but also those of the people we meet. If it works, it works, if it doesn't, it doesn't. In the All'Scone kitchen it's all about trying things out and making them work for us. Each week on the stall we would test out new flavours and watch the reactions to see what caused a stir – Lemon was the hit of summer 2012, Spicy Festive Hearts warmed plenty of bellies in December, but the Cherry and Almond has always remained the reigning champion.

Our aim with this book is to open the floodgates and show you all the opportunities presented by the British institution that is the scone. Why not mix it up and make Pistachio and Nutella Bites, or Feta, Garlic and Spring Onion scones with lashings of cream cheese and chutney? The Salted Caramel and Baileys Fancies will impress the coolest of customers, and the Smoked Cheddar and Marmite nibbles go down swimmingly with a Desperado or two.

The book is split into sweet and savoury halves and then into sub-categories: the basic recipe with variations, and then the twisted recipes that take things to a whole new level. You may get your kicks from one of the variations on our basic recipes, but if you're a show-off (like Grace) or want more of a challenge (like Liam), then head to the twisted sections, where there really is a scone for every occasion. We always try to use ingredients that are easy to get hold of or are likely to be lurking at the back of the cupboard, as this is how we started – from scratch.

Writing the book has been a steep learning curve for both of us. We have had to push the boundaries even further than we would for the stall – more elaborate recipes, more out-there ideas and more unusual flavour combinations that work as scones and aren't just novelties. We needed flavours that would excite people, that are modern but give a respectful nod to the scone of the past.

Most importantly, through many sleepless nights, after both baking failures and triumphs, and Elvis sing-alongs that helped us keep going, we have learned to have fun with our baking and ride this adventure together. We hope you enjoy using our recipes as much as we enjoyed creating them.

So go on, don your pinny, turn up Frank, Prince, Daft Punk or whoever makes up your ideal soundtrack and join the revolution … before it's All'Scone.

Liam and Grace x

SCONE KNOW-HOW

In the All'Scone kitchen we have a few ways of keeping our scones looking and tasting top dog, and we want to share them with you so that you too can have towering, megatron scones. We believe in making life easy, so follow these simple rules and you can't go far wrong.

First things first, you'll need the following vital pieces of kit to get you started:

- ♥ Timer
- ♥ Scales – We love our old rustic scales with the measurements scratched on, however digital scales may give you a more accurate reading
- ♥ Rolling pin
- ♥ Spatula or palette knife (soon to be your best friend as it will never leave your hand)
- ♥ Pastry brush (successfully stolen from your mum's baking drawer)
- ♥ Big old mixing bowl (shhhh, Mum still doesn't know we have this either)
- ♥ Cutters (plain, fluted or heart-shaped)
- ♥ Large knife
- ♥ Whisk
- ♥ Jug
- ♥ Baking tray
- ♥ Flour sprinkler (ours is super jolly)
- ♥ Your trademark pinny (or a wardrobe of pinnies for different occasions)
- ♥ Music (a fusion of sounds from Fred Astaire to Chicago will do the trick)

Next are a few pointers on your ingredients, plus a few other cheeky tips we have picked up along the way:

♥ We keep our recipes simple with solid ingredients for the mixing bowl and wet ones for the jug.

♥ For best results keep your ingredients as cold as possible, so anything that comes from the fridge should be kept in there until it's needed for mixing, especially your butter. By using cold butter, you help prevent it being absorbed by the flour and this creates sneaky little layers between the dough and butter. Then when the dough gets hot in the oven the butter melts and leaves behind small pockets of air in its place. This gives you a super-soaring scone with a flaky, buttery structure.

♥ Using a measuring spoon, the large scone quantity calls for around 6 tablespoons of buttermilk. If you're using a tablespoon from the cutlery drawer, 3 of these heaped may be sufficient.

♥ If you can't get hold of buttermilk you can use natural yoghurt mixed with a splash of milk or water to loosen it. You can also use milk that's been thickened with a good squeeze of lemon juice.

♥ There is a lot of debate as to how long you should spend kneading/chaffing (a form of kneading where the dough is folded instead of stretched, see next point) your dough. Here is our secret. Cut the wet ingredients into the dry ones using your spatula, then gently bring it together with your fingers. Work the dough in the bowl until it begins to come together, leaving the sides of the bowl clean then pop it on a floured surface. Knead or chaff the dough until the texture is just smooth, with no lumps or bumps.

♥ To chaff your dough, push the bottom of your palm into the dough a couple of times, gather the edges in and under, then flip it over and start again. You will normally need to chaff your dough 3–5 times depending whether you have big hands like Liam, or little hands like Grace.

♥ Dip your cutter into the bag of flour before cutting your scones. The scones will fall out of the cutter and won't get stuck. Be very careful when you're pulling the cutter from the dough. NEVER twist or you'll get wonky scones – which equals unhappy scones!

♥ Check the freshness of your flour! As soon as you open your flour it will start to lose its freshness. If you are using self-raising flour this also means that the raising agent inside it will start to lose its effectiveness and this will affect how well the scones rise.

♥ Learn from the texture of your finished bakes – if they taste dry you may have baked them for too long – the best thing to do is to check the scones 5 minutes before they are due to be finished. If the texture is slightly bread-like then you may have chaffed/kneaded your dough a few too many times.

♥ Fan ovens tend to be 20°C hotter than conventional ovens (our recipes give temperatures for conventional). If you are using a fan oven, set it 20°C lower and check your scones just before finishing time to see how they are getting on.

- ♥ Individual scones are baked on floured baking sheets. If your tray tends to stick, line it with baking parchment (not greaseproof paper) and they'll lift off easily.

- ♥ The recipes in the basic sweet and savoury scone sections will yield 6 scones with a 9-cm/3½-inch cutter, 7 scones (plus a 'runt') with an 8-cm/3-inch cutter and eight scones (plus a 'runt') with a 7-cm/2¾-inch cutter. The twisted recipes are slightly different so we've specified how many these will make or serve.

HOW TO SERVE YOUR SCONES

When serving your skyscraper scones, don't be afraid to get creative in your presentation. At All'Scone we have two ways of serving our basic scones and their variations. The traditional way: cut the scone in half widthways and slather both halves separately with the toppings of your choice (perfect for a self-indulgent moment with a super-large brew). The twisted way: cut the scone in half widthways, put one topping on one side and another topping on the other side, then sandwich the two halves back together – you then have a scone to go that's perfect for packed lunches, a takeaway snack or just an alternative way to serve your creations!

STORAGE

Scones have a relatively short shelf life and so are best eaten within 2–3 days. When you're not scoffing them down we recommend you store your scones in an airtight container away from direct sunlight, somewhere cool. If you can, avoid popping them in the fridge (unless there are large quantities of cream involved) as this can harden the scones.

FREEZING

If, for whatever reason, you don't manage to chomp your way through your scone-baking accomplishments, they can easily be frozen for up to a month. Freeze on the day of baking, undecorated, either wrapped in cling film or bagged up. To defrost, take them out a couple of hours before you plan to serve them. They will still taste great, but our recommendation once fully thawed is to scoff them warm (see below). Served with generous helpings of cream and jam, custard, cream cheese and chutney – whatever is needed – your scones will be fully brought back to life.

REHEATING

We love our scones warm with lashing of clotted cream and jam, butter or cream cheese and chutney if you have a savoury tooth and we know you will too! If you want to reheat your scones then you can warm one scone in a microwave for 15–20 seconds or in a preheated oven on a low heat (180°C/350°F/gas mark 4) for 2–5 minutes.

SWEET SCONES

You can't beat a traditional plain scone served with clotted cream and jam, and our plain recipe has been the one that we have spent the most time perfecting. We built the other flavours around this basic recipe. What's our favourite flavour, we hear you ask? Cherry and Almond, every time.

BASIC SWEET SCONE DOUGH

Our basic sweet scone dough is our staple recipe to which you can add your favourite flavours, something we do a lot of on the stall. We've suggested some of our variations, but you could add whatever you fancy.

FOR THE RADIO
'I Wanna Be Your Lover', Prince

FOR THE BOWL
450g/3⅔ cups self-raising flour, plus extra for dusting
175g/1½ sticks butter, fresh from the fridge (warm butter stops scones
    from rising, boo) and cut into small lumps
2 large pinches of salt
75g/heaped ⅓ cup golden caster (superfine) sugar
1 tsp custard powder

FOR THE JUG
2 large eggs
6 tbsp buttermilk, plus extra for brushing

Preheat the oven to 190°C/375°F/gas mark 5. Don your pinny, whack on Sinatra and grab your bowl.

Put the flour, butter and salt in a large bowl and rub together, using your fingers, until the mixture resembles fine breadcrumbs (or just mix it all up in a blender if you're feeling lazy). Ensure all the butter is fully broken down so that you don't get gloopy lumps in your finished scones. Add the sugar and custard powder.

In the jug, whisk together the eggs and buttermilk until airy and fluffy – you want the mixture as light as possible so that your scones rise to skyscraper proportions.

Time to mix it up. Pour the contents of the jug into the bowl and, using a spatula, gently mix the whole lot together. It will start to form into a dough, but will need finishing off with your hands, so get stuck in. If it seems too dry, add another tablespoon of buttermilk. If it's too wet, add a sprinkle of flour. Gently fold the dough until it comes away cleanly from the sides of the bowl and is more or less one large lump of yumminess.

Pop the dough on to a lightly floured surface and chaff gently until it becomes smooth (see page 14–15 for chaffing techniques). Grab a lightly floured rolling pin and roll out the dough until you have a thickness of approximately 3cm/1¼ inches – no less or they won't be happy. Gently cut out your scones.

Place your scones on a lightly floured baking tray and brush them with buttermilk. Sift some flour over them all (like it's snowing) then pop them on the middle shelf of the oven. Set your timer for 20 minutes (they may need 5 or so minutes more) and make sure you do not open the oven door until they are golden brown.

Shimmy the baked scones on to a cooling rack and resist eating them for about 10 minutes so that they cool down just enough for you to try. The rest will be fine to eat for the next 2 days, or pop them in the freezer if you haven't eaten them by then!

CHERRY AND ALMOND HEARTS

This is the scone that started it all. We came up with these little beauties when we started dating and they became a firm favourite among friends and family. They are still our bestseller on the market stall (and will always be Grace's ultimate scone!) When you bite into them you should be reminded of the childhood taste of wholesome cherry bakewells – if this is the case, then you have succeeded in your mission.

FOR THE RADIO
'Cheek to Cheek', Frank Sinatra

FOR THE BOWL
450g/3⅔ cups self-raising flour, plus extra for dusting
175g/1½ sticks butter, fresh from the fridge and cut into small lumps
2 large pinches of salt
75g/heaped ⅓ cup golden caster (superfine) sugar
1 tsp custard powder
a super-large handful of finely chopped glacé cherries (about
    100g/3½oz cherries)

FOR THE JUG
2 large eggs
6 tbsp buttermilk, plus extra for brushing
2–3 tsp almond essence

FOR THE TABLE
strawberry jam
clotted cream

Preheat the oven to 190°C/375°F/gas mark 5.

Put the flour, butter and salt in a large bowl and rub together, using your fingers, until the mixture resembles fine breadcrumbs, ensuring the butter is fully broken down. Alternatively you can do this stage in a food processor. Stir in the sugar, custard powder and finely chopped cherries, making sure the cherries are completely incorporated into the mixture (you'll need to rub the chopped cherries into the mixture – those sneaky badgers like to stick together).

In a jug, whisk the eggs, buttermilk and almond essence until airy and fluffy. Next step – which is very important – take a good whiff of the jug mixture. You are aiming for an almond slap across the face – if you don't get this, add more essence. Add this mixture to the dry ingredients in the bowl and mix gently with a spatula to combine, finishing off the dough with your fingers. If it seems too dry, add another tablespoon of buttermilk. If it's too wet, add a sprinkle of flour – ideally it should be sticky for a short while, then it should seem a bit too dry before finally coming together. Not high maintenance at all then! Gently fold the dough until it comes away cleanly from the sides of the bowl, nice and neatly.

On a lightly floured surface, chaff the dough, being careful not to overwork it, then roll out to a 3cm/1¼-inch thickness. Cut out your scones (don't twist, this is vital! Your scones will not be happy if you do). Brush with a little buttermilk and dust with flour.

Bake in the oven for approximately 25 minutes, or until the scones are golden brown. A good tip for checking that they're cooked through is to lightly tap their base; you should get a hollow sound – Liam does this with a very serious face. Leave to cool a little bit on a cooling rack then serve warm with lashings of strawberry jam and tons of clotted cream! Ooo, and a nice pot of Russian Caravan tea.

SPICY FESTIVE HEARTS

This scone is perfect for when you're feeling festive and need your heart warming – at any time of the year! With one bite of these there will be a full-on Christmas party happening in your mouth. We have been known to make these as early as August (Christmas is big in our house) whilst listening to Michael Bublé … Shhhh, Liam!

FOR THE RADIO
'It's Beginning to Look a Lot Like Christmas', Michael Bublé

FOR THE BOWL
450g/3⅔ cups self-raising flour, plus extra for dusting
175g/1½ sticks butter, fresh from the fridge and cut into small lumps
2 large pinches of salt
75g/heaped ⅓ cup golden caster (superfine) sugar
1 tsp custard powder
2 tbsp ground cinnamon, plus extra for dusting
2 tsp ground nutmeg
2 tsp ground ginger
2 tsp ground allspice

FOR THE JUG
2 large eggs
6–8 tbsp buttermilk, plus extra for brushing

FOR THE TABLE
clotted or brandy cream

Preheat the oven to 190°C/375°F/gas mark 5.

Put the flour, butter and salt in a large bowl and rub together, using your fingers, until the mixture resembles fine breadcrumbs, or you can whack it all in a food blender and let the hard work be done for you – either way, ensure that the butter has been fully incorporated. Throw in the sugar, custard powder and spices and mix to combine.

Whisk the eggs and buttermilk into a frenzy until airy and fluffy. Add this mixture to the dry ingredients in the bowl and mix gently with a spatula to combine, finishing off the dough with your fingers. If it seems too dry, add another tablespoon of buttermilk. If it's too wet, add a sprinkle of flour. Gently fold the dough until it comes away cleanly from the sides of the bowl.

Chaff the dough, being careful not to overwork it. This dough can be quite dry due to the extra ingredients, so don't be afraid to add a little more buttermilk if necessary. Once you have a smooth dough, roll it out to a 3cm/1¼-inch thickness and carefully cut out your scones. Are you getting the smell of Christmas yet?

Place the scones on a lightly dusted baking tray, brush with buttermilk and dust with flour and ground cinnamon. Pop in the oven for 25–30 minutes, or until the dough has turned a darker brown. Whilst they're in the oven, turn Bublé up and write your Christmas card list. When they're done, transfer to a wire rack to cool.

These scones taste delicious served with clotted cream, but if you're feeling particularly extravagant, try brandy cream instead. Maybe pop on a few Christmas carols whilst indulging? This may be a step too far for some.

THE LITTLE BOOK OF SCONES

ZINGY LEMON SCONES
WITH MASCARPONE AND LEMON CURD

This little scone is packed with zesty lemon flavour that reminds us of our early days on the market. It was springtime and these lemon bobby dazzlers went down a treat!

The addition of lemon juice means this scone needs less buttermilk than the standard recipe and the dough will be denser. They may need slightly longer in the oven than the other recipes as a result.

FOR THE RADIO
'Tutti Frutti', Elvis Presley

FOR THE BOWL
450g/3⅔ cups self-raising flour, plus extra for dusting
2 large pinches of salt
175g/1½ sticks butter, fresh from the fridge and cut into small lumps
75g/heaped ⅓ cup golden caster (superfine) sugar
1 tsp custard powder
zest of 1 lemon

FOR THE JUG
2 large eggs
3–4 tbsp buttermilk, plus extra for brushing
juice of 1 lemon

FOR THE PLATE
mascarpone cheese
lemon curd
clotted cream (optional)

Preheat the oven to 190°C/375°F/gas mark 5.

In a large bowl, rub together the flour, salt and butter with your fingers until it looks like breadcrumbs, ensuring all of the butter has been rubbed in. You could do this in a food processor to speed things up if you wish. Next add the sugar, custard powder and lemon zest and mix well with your fingers to ensure the lemon is well incorporated – you don't want any cheeky clumps hanging about in there!

Whisk together the wet ingredients in the jug until airy and fluffy. Pour this into the bowl and gently fold together with a spatula. Finish it off with your hands, easing it off the sides of the bowl. This dough will seem quite wet so you may need to add a tad more flour at this point in order to bring the dough together.

Tip on to a lightly floured surface and chaff gently, being careful not to overwork the dough. Roll out to fractionally less than a 3-cm/1¼-inch thickness. It may seem quite dense but do not fear – this is a side effect of the lemon juice you added to the dough.

Cut out your scones and transfer to a lightly floured baking tray. Brush them with buttermilk and dust with flour. Bake in the oven for 25–30 minutes then transfer to a wire rack to cool.

These fresh and zesty scones are perfect in spring, served warm with a generous spread of mascarpone topped with lemon curd. Maybe with some extra clotted cream? We reckon you can't go far wrong with extra cream.

A tip for lemons: roll your lemon on the work surface or pop it in the microwave for 10 seconds and you'll be able to squeeze more juice out of your lemon. To juice it, hold your hand, palm up, above the jug with your fingers slightly spread. Squeeze the lemon over it – your hand will catch the pips and the juice will run through into the jug.

PRALINE SCONES

This scone is super-easy to make. When making praline go for 1-part nuts to 2-parts sugar and then you can make as much or as little as you like. For 6 large scones we use 100g of sugar to 60g of nuts. Some say not to stir the sugar as it crystallises but we do as it speeds up the process and covers the nuts better – see how you get on. Praline can be made from any nut but pecans, almonds and hazelnuts tend to make the tastiest ones. We have used hazelnut as they give a strong nutty flavour and remind us of chocolate seashells. Alternatively you can buy blanched almonds in most supermarkets, which give a more subtle taste.

Makes 12–14 scones

FOR THE RADIO
'I Heard it Through the Grapevine', Marvin Gaye

FOR THE PRALINE
100g/½ cup caster (superfine) sugar
60g/⅓ cup blanched hazelnuts, or unblanched ones plus
   1 tsp bicarbonate of soda (baking soda), and you can do
   it yourself (see method)
a little vegetable oil, for greasing

FOR THE BOWL
450g/3⅔ cups self-raising flour, plus extra for dusting
2 large pinches of salt
175g/1½ sticks butter, fresh from the fridge and cut into small lumps
75g/heaped ⅓ cup golden caster (superfine) sugar
1 tsp custard powder

FOR THE JUG

2 large eggs
5–6 tbsp buttermilk, plus extra for brushing
dark chocolate, at least 70% cocoa solids, for grating

First prepare your nuts. If you are using blanched nuts skip this step. If not, blanch your nuts in a shallow pan of boiling water with a teaspoon of bicarbonate of soda. This helps to remove the skins and takes away the bitterness. After 2–3 minutes take them out of the pan, run them under cold water then rub off the skins with a clean cloth.

Pour the caster sugar and hazelnuts into a saucepan over a medium heat. As the sugar melts, coat the nuts with it and repeat this process until the sugar is clear and dissolved. Take the pan off the heat and tip the mixture on to some oiled baking parchment or oiled kitchen foil and allow it to cool into a sugary nut brittle – it will smell divine!

Break up the praline and blend it in a blender until it's very fine. Alternatively smash it in between some cling film with a rolling pin or in a pestle and mortar. Set aside and try to leave it alone (the smell is amazing!) until it is needed. Preheat the oven to 190°C/375°F/gas mark 5.

In a large bowl, mix together the flour, salt and butter, using your fingers. You want to be rubbing the butter into the flour until it has fully broken down and looks like breadcrumbs – no large unwanted lumps of butter, thank you. You can do all of this in a food processor if you wish. Stir in the blended praline, sugar and custard powder.

In the jug, whisk together the eggs and buttermilk. You want it to be as airy as possible – get stuck in with some elbow grease! Then pour this into the bowl and, using a spatula, gently mix together. It will start to form into a dough, but will need finishing off with your hands, so get stuck in. You may need to add a tad more buttermilk if it seems too dry, or slightly more flour if it is too wet. It will not come together immediately though, so be patient with it. Gently fold the dough until it comes away cleanly from the sides of the bowl and you have a large lump of dough that you can hold safely in one hand.

Pop the dough on to a lightly floured surface and chaff gently. Just do this a few times, until you have a super smooth dough with little to no cracks, be careful not to end up with a dough that is too elastic – this will affect the rise of these praline goodies.

Grab a lightly floured rolling pin and roll out the dough to a thickness of approximately 3cm/1¼ inches – no thinner or you will have sad scones that will not rise. Dip a 4-cm/1½-inch cutter in the flour (to stop the dough sticking to it) and gently cut out your scones – don't twist them! Though you can always do a spot of twisting yourself while you wait for them to bake …

Place your scones on a lightly floured baking tray and brush them with buttermilk. Sift some flour over them all then pop them on the middle shelf of the oven. Put on a decent playlist, twist and shout a bit and after 20–25 minutes they should be ready, looking well risen and golden brown on top.

Once the scones are out of the oven and have been cooled on a wire rack, grate some dark chocolate over the tops. We go for a South American dark chocolate that's more than 70% cocoa to give them a bittersweet kick. Feast on these with lots of clotted cream and a cafetière of Columbian coffee whilst reading the papers.

RASPBERRY SCONES WITH VANILLA AND LYCHEE CREAM

These little ones have a surprising taste to them that's not what you'd expect. The raspberry lurks in the dough while the cream has a wonderful, sugary body to it. Lychee was new territory for us when we created this recipe and we're so glad we found it – this cream will be used many a time!

Makes 12–14

FOR THE RADIO
'Raspberry Beret', Prince

FOR THE BOWL
450g/3⅔ cups self-raising flour, plus extra for dusting
2 large pinches of salt
175g/1½ sticks butter, fresh from the fridge and cut into small lumps
75g/heaped ⅓ cup golden caster (superfine) sugar
1 tsp custard powder
90g/3oz fresh raspberries, washed
1 heaped tsp baking powder

FOR THE JUG
2 medium eggs
5–6 tbsp buttermilk

FOR THE CREAM
200ml/¾ cup + 4 tsp double (heavy) cream
2 tsp caster (superfine) sugar
12 lychees, finely chopped
1 tsp vanilla extract

Preheat the oven to 190°C/375°F/gas mark 5.

Put the flour, salt and butter into a food processor and whiz until the mixture resembles breadcrumbs. Alternatively put all the ingredients into a bowl and rub the butter in with your fingers – either way, make sure that the butter is fully broken down and all the ingredients are fully mixed together.

Tip the mixture into a large bowl if you're not already there. Stir in the sugar, custard powder, raspberries and baking powder.

In a jug, whisk together the eggs and buttermilk until light and bubbly, then pour this into the dry mixture in the bowl. Grab your spatula and fold the mixture to bring everything together roughly, then finish off with your hands – you should be able to feel the raspberries squishing as they pop. We love the bright red colour that leaks into the dough. This is what you want as the flavour will spread throughout the dough and give your scones a gorgeous pink colour when baked. Throw your spatula aside and finish off the dough by chaffing it gently with your hands on a lightly floured surface until it becomes smooth.

Roll out your dough with a lightly floured rolling pin to approximately 2.5cm/1 inch, then begin to cut out the scones. These are smaller than our other basic scones – keep them heart shaped if you wish, but use a cutter that is approximately 4cm/1½ inch in diameter. Due to the dough being so wet they will not rise well if cut too large. Dip the cutter into the bag of flour before using it to stop the dough sticking and disfiguring the scones ... You may need to dip it in for almost every scone – this is normal!

Brush the tops of your scones with buttermilk and dust with flour as usual then bake for about 15–20 minutes. Transfer to a wire rack to cool.

Now make your cream. Whisk the cream using an electric whisk (you'll be there all day if you try to do it by hand), and gradually add the sugar. Whisk until it forms stiff peaks. Add the vanilla extract just as you are finishing the whisking.

When the cream is fully whisked stir in the chopped lychees, then pop it all in the fridge until the scones have completely cooled.

When they are ready, halve the scones horizontally and fill generously with the lychee and vanilla cream. Keep in the fridge until you are ready to serve them, as this will keep the cream super-fresh. Serve on fine china with a pretty pot of Earl- or Lady Grey tea.

ORANGE AND CARDAMOM SCONES

These scones have a light, subtle flavour that's refreshing and very moreish.
The icing drizzled on the top gives them an extra dose of sugar sweetness.
Adjust the amount of cardamom to your taste – we use 4 teaspoons as we
like the flavour to come through as much as the orange, but have a play
around and see what you prefer.

FOR THE RADIO
'Loaded', Primal Scream

FOR THE BOWL
450g/3⅔ cups self-raising flour, plus extra for dusting
175g/1½ sticks butter, cut into small lumps and fresh from the fridge
75g/heaped ⅓ cup golden caster (superfine) sugar
2 large pinches of salt
1 tsp custard powder
zest of 1 large orange
1–4 heaped tsp ground cardamom

FOR THE JUG
juice of ½ large orange (approx. 50ml)
2 large eggs
2 tbsp buttermilk

FOR THE ICING
4 tsp freshly squeezed orange juice
¾ tsp ground cardamom
4 tbsp icing sugar

Preheat the oven to 190°C/375°F/gas mark 5. Lightly dust a baking tray.

Put the flour, butter and salt in a large mixing bowl and rub together, using your fingers, until the mixture resembles fine breadcrumbs (or just pop it all in a blender if you like). Ensure all the butter is fully incorporated, then add the sugar, custard powder, orange zest and cardamom. Again use your fingers to rub the mixture together and to combine all of the ingredients, so you get an even flavour throughout.

In the jug, whisk together the orange juice, eggs and buttermilk until light and airy.

Pour the egg mixture into the mixing bowl and gently mix it all up with a spatula. When it starts to form large clumps, dramatically throw your spatula to one side, roll up your sleeves and bring the dough together with your hands, pressing it to the sides of the bowl and rolling it around a tad. It will take a short while for it to come clean off the sides of the bowl, but if you feel like you need a helping hand, add a touch more flour or buttermilk accordingly. Carry on bringing the dough together until it is one lump of dough that can easily be lifted out of the bowl and on to ...

A lightly floured surface. Chaff gently until it becomes smooth, then roll out the dough until it measures 3cm/1¼ inches in depth – no more, no less. Gently cut out your scones, avoiding the dreaded twist (the consequences of this fatal mistake could cost you a poor rise in your scones – something none of us want.)

Lightly dust a baking tray and place your scones on it. Brush with a little buttermilk, then grab your flour duster once more and give them a good sprinkling over the top. Place them on the middle shelf of the oven for 20–25 minutes.

Whilst the scones are busy baking you can make your icing drizzle. In a medium-sized bowl throw in the orange juice, ground cardamom and icing sugar. Whisk it all up until it becomes smooth and consistent, then try your best to leave to one side until your super-scones are done. Okay, maybe just a little finger-dip to taste ...

Once the scones are ready and smelling amazing (give them a tap on the underneath to check – you're listening out for a hollow sound with a firm base) pop them on a cooling rack and, using a teaspoon, drizzle immediately with your icing. Leave to cool until the icing has set then gobble them down with the trusted toppings of clotted cream, lashings of butter and chopped fresh fruit, such as kiwi or strawberries ... More please!

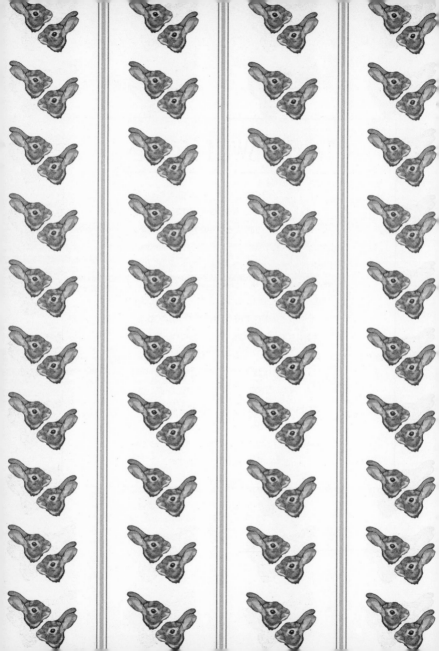

TWISTED SWEET SCONES

At All'Scone we love a good scone.
But over time we've realised that the humble
scone dough can be a vehicle for many
different flavours, textures and dishes,
making it a lot more adventurous than
you might think. In this section we will
introduce you to a few of our favourite
ways of using this adaptable dough:
the range of fancies will look deceptively
dainty to your non-scone-loving friends,
and puddings recreated, such as the
Monkey Butter Pudding and Scone
Roly Poly, are simple, twisted versions
of the originals. All of them are fun to
make and show just how flexible our
loveable scone can be.

WHOLEMEAL APPLE, CINNAMON AND SULTANA LOAF

When he was a nipper Liam ate lots of his gran's fruitcakes, pies and loaves. This cinnamon loaf is inspired by her baking and it's extremely delicious on a crisp, sunny autumn day.

If you can soak your sultanas in apple juice overnight before you start baking it will add moisture to your loaf and give it an extra boost of flavour. No worries if you don't have time though, it will still be super-yummy if you throw the fruit in dry.

Serves 6

FOR THE RADIO
'Every Little Thing She Does is Magic', The Police

FOR THE BOWL
225g/1¾ cups self-raising flour
75g/5 tbsp butter, plus a little extra for greasing
a pinch of salt
1 tsp custard powder
40g/2 tbsp + 1 tsp caster (superfine) sugar
100g/½ cup dried sultanas (golden raisins)
50g/⅓ cup peeled grated apple
4 tsp ground cinnamon

FOR THE JUG
1 large egg
4–5 tbsp milk

FOR THE TIN
flour, for dusting
dash of milk, for brushing
½ apple, sliced, for decorating
demerara sugar, for dusting
ground cinnamon, for sprinkling

Preheat the oven to 200°C/400°F/gas mark 6. Grab a 900g/2lb loaf tin and lightly butter then dust the inside with flour.

In a blender, whizz together the flour, butter and salt until the mixture looks like fine breadcrumbs. Transfer to a large bowl and add in the custard powder, caster sugar, sultanas, grated apple and cinnamon. Make sure it's all mixed in well by using your hands – then you can fully segregate the grated apple as it likes to stick together.

In a jug, whisk together the egg and milk until it's light and airy and pour it into the mixture in the bowl.

Mix all of the ingredients together with a spatula, then tip on to a floured surface and finish it off by chaffing with your hands to make a smooth dough (see pages 14–15 for chaffing techniques). Once the dough is smooth, gradually roll it into a large sausage shape with your hands. You want it to be approximately 25–30cm/10–12 inches long and 6–8cm/2–3 inches high, just the perfect size to fit into your tin.

Gently place your loaf in the tin (there should be a little space at either end), brush with milk and decorate with the sliced apple. You can be as creative as you like, but a simple, pretty way is to overlap the slices diagonally down the length of the loaf. Dust with demerara sugar and finish with a generous sprinkling of ground cinnamon to top it all off.

Bake in the middle of the oven for 30–35 minutes or until the top of the loaf is firm to the touch. A handy tip is to push a sharp knife through the loaf – if it comes out clean, it's ready. When your loaf is baked, transfer it to a wire rack to cool … Don't even think about nibbling the edges!

Serve slices of this loaf warm with generous amounts of full-fat butter (as you would with a malt loaf) and a hearty brew!

TRIPLE-THREAT SCONE CREAM CAKE

This scone cake is the ultimate calorific treat – made with double, clotted and whipped creams, we dare you to see how many slices you can scoff before you end up rolling around on the floor! The fig topping complements the fig jam centre, which really brings the whole sha-bang together. This is perfect for a summer party where you want to turn heads – and fill people up pronto!

Serves 8

FOR THE RADIO
'Summer Song', Leddra Chapman

FOR THE BOWL
350g/2¾ cups self-raising flour, plus a little extra for dusting
1 tsp baking powder
a pinch of salt
50g/3 tbsp + 1 tsp butter, plus a little extra for greasing
25g/⅛ cup caster (superfine) sugar
1 tsp custard powder

FOR THE JUG
2 large eggs
75ml/¼ cup + 1 tbsp clotted cream
75ml/¼ cup + 1 tbsp double (heavy) cream, plus a little extra
    for brushing
1 tsp vanilla extract

FOR THE ASSEMBLY
fig jam, for filling the cake
200ml/¾ cup + 4 tsp whipped cream
25g/⅛ cup caster (superfine) sugar
50g/⅔ cup desiccated (unsweetened shredded) coconut
5 figs, washed and each cut into 8 segments

Preheat the oven to 220°C/425°F/gas mark 7. Grease and dust a round 23-cm/9-inch springform cake tin.

In a bowl, blend together the flour, baking powder, salt and butter until it looks like breadcrumbs, or whack it all in a blender for a few seconds. Add the sugar and custard powder and mix together well.

In a jug whisk together the eggs, clotted cream, double cream and vanilla extract – it should smell amazing! We can never eat enough cream in the All'Scone kitchen.

Add the contents of the jug to the bowl and bring it all together to form a dough, until it comes clean away from the sides of the bowl. Finish off on a lightly floured work surface until smooth, chaffing your dough into perfection.

Pop the dough in the baking tin and, using the palm of your hand, gently push it out until the whole of the base is covered and the dough is flat on top. Don't worry about it looking perfectly even, when it rises in the oven it will level itself out. Brush with a little double cream (told you – we lurve the cream) and place on the middle shelf of the oven for 30–35 minutes. Once cooked transfer to a wire rack to cool completely.

Once cooled, slice the cold cake in half horizontally. Slather the fig jam over the bottom layer and gently sandwich the cake back together, letting the jam squidge cheekily out of the sides.

Grab your electric whisk and start whisking up the double cream for the top, adding the caster sugar and coconut as you go, until the mixture firms up. You want it to form stubborn stiff peaks, so if you turn the bowl upside down nothing would fall out. Go on, we dare you – give it a try!

Spoon the cream on the top of the scone cake, spreading it out to the edges with a spatula or the back of a spoon. Lastly, decorate with the fig segments – you should have enough to form 2 overlapping circles, spiralling smaller each time and finishing off with a few segments in the middle as a fancy flourish. You don't have to use this decorative idea though, feel free to be as creative as you wish! Only once all of the fig segments have been arranged can you lick the spoon from the bowl of cream. Place on a cake stand so your cake can get the full attention it deserves.

Serve this cake under the dappled shade of a tree in mid-summer with a chilled jug of homemade lemonade, during a break in a game of lawn tennis or something similar. Failing that, serve inside on a rainy day with the heating on full blast and a big mug of builder's brew.

PISTACHIO AND NUTELLA FANCIES

We initially served this recipe as a large scone but soon realised its potential for showing off! We made smaller ones that can be stacked and presented in any way you like – or just gobbled one by one! Place 6 fancies in a cake box, tie with ribbon and you have the perfect gift.

Makes 15–20 fancies

FOR THE RADIO
'Gettin' Jiggy Wit It', Will Smith

FOR THE BOWL
225g/1¾ cups self-raising flour, plus extra for dusting
75g/5 tbsp butter, cut into chunks
1 tsp custard powder
40g/2 tbsp + 1 tsp caster (superfine) sugar
a super-large pinch of salt
100g/¾ cup pistachios, shelled
3 tsp cocoa powder

FOR THE JUG
1 large egg
4 tbsp buttermilk
2 tsp Nutella or similar hazelnut chocolate spread

FOR THE ASSEMBLY
clotted cream
100–150g/⅓ cup + 1 tbsp–scant ⅔ cup Nutella or similar
    hazelnut chocolate spread

Preheat the oven to 190°C/375°F/gas mark 5.

Blend the flour, butter, custard powder, sugar and salt either in a blender or in a bowl using your fingers, rubbing the mixture together until it forms a texture similar to breadcrumbs.

Pop the pistachios into a food processor and blend until well ground. Place half the ground pistachios in a shallow dish and set aside. Add the other half to the bowl full of mixture, along with the cocoa powder and mix to combine. Be generous with the cocoa powder – you want these tiny tasters to really pack a punch.

In a jug, whisk together the egg, buttermilk and 2 teaspoons of the Nutella. This may seem a tad tricky to begin with as the spread seems quite stubborn, but see it out and get the better of it. Once fully whisked together, add slowly to the dry ingredients in the bowl and mix together with a spatula.

When the dough starts to form, tip it on to a lightly floured work surface and chaff until you have a smooth dough. Roll it out until it is approximately 2.5cm/1¾ inches thick, then take a 2- or 3-cm/¾- or 1¼-inch heart-shaped cutter, or the rim of a shot glass dipped in flour, and cut out about 15–20 fancies (try not to rework the dough when rolling out as this will affect the height of your fancies).

Place your fancies on a lightly floured baking tray. Pop in the oven for 15 minutes, then transfer to a cooling rack to cool completely. Once cooled, cut each fancy in half widthways and sandwich the two halves together with clotted cream. Set aside. DO NOT EAT YET! This part is so hard.

Now you need to melt the remaining Nutella. To make a bain-marie, bring 500ml/2 cups water to a simmer in a pan over a medium heat. Place a glass bowl over the pan, ensuring the base does not touch the bottom of the pan, but hovers comfortably in the water.

TWISTED SWEET SCONES

Spoon the remaining spread into the bowl and stir slowly until it runs easily off the spoon… Total gorgeousness!

Now for the fun part – decorating your fancies! You'll need the ground pistachios you set aside earlier. Grab a skewer and stick it right through the middle of one of your fancies. Dip the fancy in the melted chocolate spread and gently roll it around (a butter knife is usually a handy tool at this point). Take the fancy out and roll it in the ground pistachios. Carefully place the coated fancy on a plate, remove the skewer, and gently cover the hole with a pinch of pistachio, et voilà! You've made your first fancy!

When the rest of the fancies are decorated, pop the plate in a cool place, preferably not the fridge as this will harden them, and leave to cool for at least 30 minutes (sometimes we can't wait that long!) before eating.

RED VELVET SCONE FANCIES WITH GLITTERED ICED ROSES

These fancies are made in the traditional way using beetroot. Alongside the cream cheese filling the taste is quite subtle and is the perfect accompaniment to a sophisticated social gathering. If you make circular fancies, you will have some leftover scone slab, but you can mash it up with some double cream, sprinkle chopped chocolate over the top and have a perfect freezable dessert!

Makes 16 fancies

FOR THE RADIO
'Love is a Losing Game', Amy Winehouse

FOR THE BOWL
350g/2¾ cups self-raising flour, plus extra for dusting
a pinch of salt
40g/3 tbsp butter
100g/½ cup caster (superfine) sugar
1 heaped tsp baking powder
75g/¾ cup cocoa powder
1 tsp instant coffee
175g/6oz cooked peeled beetroot in natural juices, finely diced or
    blended (don't allow the beetroot to liquidise or it will be hard
    to incorporate into the mixture – you want fine chunks)

FOR THE JUG
1 large egg
150ml/⅔ cup double (heavy) cream, plus extra for brushing
100ml/⅓ cup + 1 tbsp milk

FOR THE TOP
200g/7oz cream cheese
50ml/3 tbsp + 1 tsp double (heavy) cream
75g/heaped ⅓ cup caster (superfine) sugar

FOR THE ROSES
125g/4½oz ready-to-roll fondant icing
a drop of red food colouring
edible glitter, in whichever colour you prefer (silver is our favourite)

First things first – if you have not managed to end up with cooked beetroot, do not fret – whole beetroot can easily be simmered in a pan of cold water until soft. This should take around 20–30 minutes, depending on how big they are. Once soft, drain and set aside.

Preheat the oven to 190°C/375°F/gas mark 5. Lightly grease a 24 x 24-cm/9½ x 9½-inch oven dish.

Blend the flour, salt and butter in a blender (or use your fingers) until the mixture resembles breadcrumbs. Add the sugar, baking powder, cocoa powder and coffee. Mix together well. Add the beetroot and stir to combine.

In a large jug whisk together the egg, double cream and milk. Fold this mixture into the dry mix, using a spatula, until the dough comes together. Keep the dough in the bowl and fold over a couple of times; be careful not to get too eager and don't overdo it.

Once you have folded it over a few times, tip it (no need for a rolling pin for this one) into your oven dish (it needn't be perfect as the dough will fill it out when it rises). Brush the top with double cream, dust with a little flour and pop in the oven for about 35–45 minutes, or until you can retract a knife from the middle with no residue on it. Put your feet up, have a cuppa and wait! Or you could make your icing roses.

To make your icing roses, take the fondant icing and knead it firmly in your hands to soften it up. Make a small well in the middle of the icing and pour a drop of food colouring into it then knead it into the icing. This can be tricky as the colouring likes to try to escape, but swiftness is key! Just keep kneading it in carefully until you get a marble effect.

Split the icing into quarters, then roll out each piece with your hands to form a sausage shape approximately 1-cm/½-inch thick. Cut off slices that measure 5mm/¼ inch; you'll need 72 slices eventually, but we find it easier to deal with 18 petals at a time (6 petals make one rose).

Take a piece of cling film and place 6 slices on one half in the shape of a flower, leaving a good gap in between each one. Fold the other half of the cling film over the slices and press each one out gently with your thumb, creating a thin petal. Repeat with all 6 slices, then carefully peel off the top layer of cling film and, very gently, tease a petal off the cling film with your nail. Start to roll the petal around itself until it is fully rolled up, then curl one edge back ever so slightly to resemble a rose petal.

Peel off another petal and roll it round the first one, placing the middle of the second petal over the join of the first one. Don't roll them too tightly or you won't get the full rose effect. Carry on rolling the petals around each other, pushing back the tips, until you have used all 6 petals. You should by now have a beautiful rose! Carefully pinch the bottom off and set aside. Repeat until you have 16 roses – it is a good idea to have some calming music on whilst you complete this task, as it can get quite fiddly – no raving tunes here, Liam!

Once baked, take the dish out of the oven and leave to cool slightly. Once it has cooled a bit, carefully transfer the scone to a cooling rack. Leave to cool completely.

In a large bowl, mix together the cream cheese, double cream and caster sugar with a wooden spoon. You want the mixture to be as light and fluffy as possible, so the aim is to treat it as you would when mixing ingredients for a sponge cake – quick, light movements. Taste to test and add more sugar if needed – you want it to be sweet with a subtle taste of cream cheese in the background.

When the slab is fully cooled, put it on a clean surface and cut it horizontally in half with a sharp knife. Grab your bowl of cream cheese and slather all over the bottom half, then sandwich the top half back on – put on just enough for the cream to peek out of the sides, but not spill over. Use the rest of the cream to cover the top then cut your slab into 16 squares or, alternatively, make circular fancies using a 4cm/1½-inch cutter dunked into the bag of flour. You will have to fill and top these ones individually – they just take a little more time, but are equally attractive.

Very gently, press your roses on to the top of your scones. Repeat until you have roses on top of all of your scones, then gather together and blow a little edible glitter over the top. Ta da! Present them how you wish, but whatever you do, make sure these little beauties are the centre of attention!

*You can buy fondant icing in many colours, though it can be tricky to find in most supermarkets, so in this recipe we have included colouring. However if you manage to find some in a colour you want to use, great! Skip the food colouring.

BAILEYS AND SALTED CARAMEL FANCIES

These little bad-asses are particular favourites. The muscovado gives them a dough-like texture and the Baileys cream hits you right in the face — then the creaminess of the salted caramel brings it all back.

Makes 16 fancies

FOR THE RADIO
'I Get a Kick Out of You', Frank Sinatra

FOR THE BOWL
350g/2¾ cups self-raising flour, plus extra for dusting
100g/7 tbsp salted butter
a pinch of salt
1 tsp baking powder
100g/½ cup light brown muscovado sugar
4 level tsp grated dark chocolate

FOR THE JUG
1 large egg
200ml/¾ cup + 4 tsp double (heavy) cream, plus extra for brushing
50ml/3 tbsp + 1 tsp milk
seeds from 1 vanilla pod

FOR THE FILLING
100ml/⅓ cup + 1 tbsp double cream
1 tsp caster sugar
50ml/3 tbsp + 1 tsp Baileys
salted caramel sauce, if you can't find any, caramel sauce is fine
    with a little salt sprinkled over the top

FOR FLAIR
Maltesers, for decorating
cocoa powder, for decorating

Preheat the oven to 190°C/375°F/gas mark 5.

Blend the flour, butter and salt together in a blender. Tip into a large bowl and add the baking powder, sugar and grated chocolate. Mix well.

In a jug whisk together the egg, double cream, milk and vanilla seeds and fold into the dry mixture. Chaff together and finish off on a lightly floured surface until smooth.

Grease an oven dish (approximately 24 x 24 cm/9½ x 9½ inches) and pop the scone dough in. Push the edges of the dough out into the corners, brush with a little double cream and place in the oven for about 30–40 minutes, or until a knife comes out clean when inserted into the dough. When it is ready, set the scone aside whilst you make your filling and leave it to cool thoroughly.

To make the Baileys cream filling, throw the double cream and the sugar into a large bowl and whisk until you have a mousse. Use an electric whisk if possible, as we learnt the hard way once by doing it by hand … Fold in the Baileys and whisk again until just thick.

Once the scone slab has cooled and your cream is ready, use a 4-cm/1½-inch circular cutter and cut out 16 scones from the slab. Tip: dunk the cutter in flour before cutting out your scones to avoid any badly shaped ones.

Slice your scones in half, keeping the halves together so you don't get confused! Place a teaspoon of the salted caramel sauce on the middle of every half and spread evenly, not going over the edges. Next, add a teaspoon of your Baileys cream to every bottom half and then sandwich the scones back together. Place another teaspoon of cream on the top of each scone, gently place a Malteser on top, and dust with cocoa powder to decorate.

To keep these bad boys so fresh and so clean, store them in an airtight container. If you are planning on eating them in a couple of days' time, the cream will last up to 2 days in the fridge and so you can always assemble them on the day of eating if preferred. And don't worry, all that leftover baked scone dough doesn't have to go to waste – pop it in a large bowl, pour in some cream, even Baileys if you're feeling carefree, mash it all up, distribute into small bowls, crush some Maltesers over the top and a drizzle of salted caramel sauce and serve as a Baileys scone mess … REEEEAAALLLLYYY GOOD!

Tip – these can also be cut into squares, so as not to have any leftover scone. Simply cut the slab horizontally in half once cooled, fill with the salted caramel sauce and cream, sandwich back together, slather the top with the remaining cream and then cut into 16 squares. Place a small blob of salted caramel sauce on the top of each one, place a Malteser in the middle, dust with cocoa powder – and there you go! Square fancies, that look just as impressive.

You will have to guard these ones with your life – they go so fast when offered out at All'Scone gatherings, and that's after we've gobbled down most of them in the kitchen!

GOLDEN SYRUP ROLY POLY

The idea for this recipe came from our mutual love for the classic roly poly, and wanting to make our own version. The lemon zest gives it a nice highlight and the golden syrup works brilliantly with the dense scone dough – a lovely variation on the old classic!

Serves 6–8

FOR THE RADIO
'Roll Over Beethoven', Chuck Berry

225g/1¾ cups self-raising flour, plus extra for rolling out
75g/¾ cup shredded vegetable suet
a pinch of salt
1 tsp baking powder
1 tsp custard powder
40g/2 tbsp + 1 tsp golden caster (superfine) sugar, plus extra
    for sprinkling
zest of 1 lemon
1 egg
100ml/⅓ cup + 1 tbsp milk, plus extra for basting
3–4 serving spoons of golden syrup
a little butter, for greasing

Preheat the oven to 200°C/400°F/gas mark 6. Butter a 900g/2lb loaf tin.

In a large mixing bowl, add ALL of the ingredients except for the egg, milk and golden syrup. Stir together well either with your hands or a wooden spoon.

In a separate bowl, whisk the egg and milk together until frothy, and pour into the mixing bowl.

With a spatula, gently bring the mixture together, until it starts to come away from the sides of the bowl. (Have patience with this, as it doesn't happen straight away!)

Throw the dough on to a lightly floured surface and knead a few times, until it becomes smooth. Take care not to overwork the dough, you will know if you have as it becomes sticky and gooey again, which will affect how much it rises in the oven. If this happens, simply knead some flour into it to make it smooth again and ask it nicely to rise well …

Once the dough is smooth, flour a clean work surface or board and roll it out with a floured rolling pin, sprinkling a little extra flour on top if it is very sticky, until it is just less than 1cm/½ inch thick and approximately 30 x 24cm/12 x 9½ inches wide. Scone dough is usually baked thick, but as you will be rolling this dough it will become quite thick anyway. Any thicker and it will not bake through thoroughly – not what we want!

Now for our favourite part – to add the golden syrup! Grab your serving spoon and place 3 large dollops of syrup on to the middle of the dough. Roughly spread the syrup over the top of the dough as much as you can, leaving a border of about 2.5cm/1 inch free around the edge. This free space will ensure the syrup stays tightly rolled up and doesn't escape during baking – hopefully! You just want a thin layer of syrup, but add another spoonful if you feel you need more. (If Grace's sister were baking this the whole tin would be used up – she's always been a severe golden syrup fiend.)

Now start to roll – we find it best to start from the bottom, curling the first part of the dough in tightly, so as to get a neat, compact effect once baked. If the dough is very sticky, you may need to use a knife to peel some of it off the work surface or board and to stick it back into the roll. Don't worry though as it won't affect the rustic presentation of this baked scone. Keep rolling until you reach the end, and then seal the roly poly by pushing gently on the seam. Turn the dough so that the seam is on the bottom and then gently fold the ends underneath – you don't want any syrup leaking out of the ends!

Carefully lift the roly poly and place inside the greased loaf tin. If the roly is slightly too long, just tease it in – it will miraculously settle itself within a few seconds. Pour a little milk over the surface of the roly poly, until the milk comes up to about a quarter of the height of the pudding. This milk will be absorbed during baking which will give it a lovely moist texture!

Dust lightly with a little golden caster sugar, pop in the oven and leave to bake for 25–30 minutes. If in doubt, insert a knife into the middle of the roly poly and draw out – if it is clean the roly poly is ready. If there is any mixture on it, it needs more time.

Serve immediately with hot custard! Or, if you prefer, with cold custard – Liam insists cold custard is the way forward.

CHOCOLATEY TIFFIN BITES

In our early dating days we loved to make tiffin, so this scone is a nod to our mutual love of baking. The biscuits soften to make a big spongy scone coating with melted chocolate for an intensely tasty afternoon treat.

Makes 18

FOR THE RADIO
'Puttin' on the Ritz', Fred Astaire

225g/1¾ cups self-raising flour, plus extra for dusting
1 level tsp baking powder
75g/5 tbsp butter
a pinch of salt
40g/2 tbsp + 1 tsp caster (superfine) sugar
4 heaped tsp cocoa powder
100g/½ cup raisins
8 McVitie's Rich Tea biscuits
2 eggs
4 tbsp buttermilk
225g/8oz milk chocolate, for the covering

Preheat the oven to 190°C/375°F/gas mark 5.

Blend together the flour, baking powder, butter and salt in a blender, to form a breadcrumb-like texture. You can also do this with your hands – it takes more time, but you will get the same effect.

Add the caster sugar, cocoa powder and raisins, and roughly crumble in the biscuits. Mix it all together well.

Whisk the eggs and buttermilk together until light and airy, and add to the mixture. Bring together with a spatula, then finish off chaffing on a floured surface. You will only need to do this a couple of times, especially as this dough is quite dry and you don't want stubborn dough that won't rise.

Roll out to about 2.5cm/1 inch and cut out using a 4-cm/1 ½-inch cutter, using the smooth edge of the cutter and pulling it straight up out of the dough, as twisting it will affect how much your scones rise.

Place on a floured baking tray, dust with flour and pop in the oven for 15 minutes. When baked, take the scones out of the oven and leave on a cooling rack until completely cool.

Now is the time to melt your chocolate. To make a bain-marie, bring water to a simmer in a pan over a medium heat. Place a glass bowl over the pan, ensuring the base does not touch the bottom of the pan, but hovers comfortably above the water, otherwise the chocolate will burn.

Place the chocolate in the bowl and stir gently until it is fully melted. Be careful not to overheat it or stir it too much, as the chocolate will start to curdle*.

Once melted, keep the chocolate over the water on a low heat then pick up a scone with two forks, upside-down. Dunk it in the chocolate, just covering the topping. Place on a plate, right side up, and repeat for all the scones.

Place in the fridge for at least 20 minutes, then present in a nice tin and sieve some icing sugar over the top. Be warned – these scones are packed with flavour and can be quite sickly after a few, so be careful not to be too greedy!

* Another handy way to melt your chocolate is to pop it in the microwave for 10-second blasts, though we find that the chocolate does curdle quite fast and you don't have the same control over it.

MONKEY BUTTER PUDDINGS

When we make large batches of scones we often have lots of leftover dough that we hate to throw away. American housewives in the 1950s used balls of leftover bread dough dipped in melted butter and cinnamon then baked in a cake tin, to create what they called a Monkey Cake. People would sit and tear pieces off it to eat. We love this idea and reworked it to make a twisted version using our leftover scone dough. You can use leftover dough from sweet flavours, like we do, or make it from scratch.

Makes 8

FOR THE RADIO
'Pennies From Heaven', Louis Prima

FOR THE BOWL
175g/1¼ cups + 1 tbsp self-raising flour
1 tbsp caster (superfine) sugar
50g/3 tbsp + 1 tsp butter, plus a little extra for greasing

FOR THE JUG
2 tbsp Greek yoghurt
1 large egg

FOR THE CUSTARD
600ml/2 cups fresh vanilla custard
50ml/3 tbsp + 1 tsp Amaretto liqueur
1 banana, sliced thinly into around 24 pieces
40g/¼ cup sultanas (golden raisins)
50g/3 tbsp + 1 tsp butter, melted
1 tbsp ground cinnamon

Preheat the oven to 190°C/375°F/gas mark 5.

Put the flour, sugar and butter into a food processor and whizz until the mixture looks like breadcrumbs. Alternatively put all the ingredients into a bowl and rub the butter in with your fingers, if you want to have an easy ride.

If you've used a food processor, tip the mixture into a large bowl. Whisk together the yoghurt and egg in a jug until it becomes as light and fluffy as a cloud. Make a well in the middle of the flour mix and pour the yoghurt mixture into it. Use a spatula to bring everything together roughly, then chaff lightly in the bowl, using your hands to make a soft dough.

Using your multitasking skills next, stir 100ml/⅓ cup + 1 tbsp custard and the Amaretto together in a jug or bowl and pop to one side for later.

Grease a 12-hole muffin tin with a little butter. Put 3 slices of banana into 8 holes of the tin. The banana will be at the bottom of the tin but once baked and turned out this will actually be the top of the pudding. Spoon 1 tablespoon of Amaretto custard on top and sprinkle a few sultanas into each hole. Once this base layer has been created it's time to start the messy bit of the pudding.

In a separate bowl stir the melted butter and cinnamon together and place next to you as a little dipping station.

Tear off small pieces of the scone dough and roll into a ball roughly the size of a walnut to make around 40 balls. Once rolled, dip each ball into the melted butter mixture to cover completely and then put 5 balls into each hole of the muffin tin on top of the banana, sultanas and custard.

Move to the oven and bake for 30 minutes. You will know when the puddings are ready as they will rise and ooze out of the cake tin and start to make your mouth water. Take the tin out of the oven and place on the side to cool for 5 minutes. While this is happening you can take the remaining custard and heat if you like in a saucepan or a microwave (although Liam will have his custard cold strange boy?). Then take a small spatula or palette knife and run it round the edge of one of the puddings. Carefully upturn it onto a bowl or plate so that the top of the pudding becomes the bottom and the entire lovely banana placed at the bottom in the beginning of the process now becomes the top. Pour over a generous helping of the custard to completely cover the pudding and enjoy with a smoky mug of Lapsang souchong.

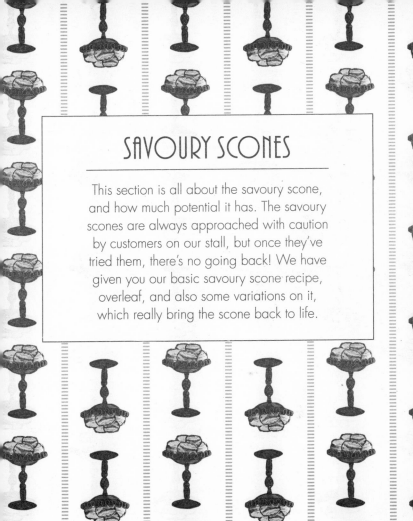

SAVOURY SCONES

This section is all about the savoury scone,
and how much potential it has. The savoury
scones are always approached with caution
by customers on our stall, but once they've
tried them, there's no going back! We have
given you our basic savoury scone recipe,
overleaf, and also some variations on it,
which really bring the scone back to life.

BASIC SAVOURY SCONE DOUGH

Scones are part of the quick bread family. When we run out of bread in the All'Scone household we often knock up a batch of these plain savoury scones. We use them to fill up our lunch boxes as sandwiches, or to have with a bowl of soup or with some cheese and chutney as a quick snack.

FOR THE RADIO
'Whatta Man', Salt-n-Pepa

FOR THE BOWL
450g/3⅔ cups self-raising flour, plus extra for dusting
175g/1½ sticks butter
40g/2 tbsp + 1 tsp golden caster (superfine) sugar
2 large pinches of salt
2 large pinches of black pepper

FOR THE JUG
2 large eggs
6 tbsp buttermilk, plus extra for brushing

Preheat the oven to 190°C/375°F/gas mark 5.

In a bowl, rub the flour and butter together gently through your fingers until the mixture resembles fine breadcrumbs. Add the sugar, salt and pepper. You can also use a food processor for this stage. Shake it all up like a polaroid picture, mixing well with your hands to finish off.

In a jug, whisk together the eggs and buttermilk until light and airy. Pour this mixture into the bowl and gently mix together with the dry ingredients, using your faithful friend, the spatula.

Work the dough in the bowl until it starts to come together, then finish with your hands until it comes away clean from the edges of the bowl. Tip on to a lightly floured surface and work through with the base of your palm three or four times, each time folding the sides in and turning over until the dough becomes smooth. (See pages 14–15 for techniques on chaffing your dough.)

Roll out the dough until it is approximately 3cm/1¼ inches thick then, using a floured round cutter, cut out your scones, being uber-cautious to avoid the temptation of twisting the cutter, which will not let your lovely scones rise.

Place your scones on a lightly floured baking tray, leaving enough space between each one for them to spread. Brush each one with buttermilk and dust with flour. Bake on the middle shelf of the oven for 20–25 minutes, or until the tops are golden brown.

These scones are delicious by themselves or with cream cheese and chutney, though we strongly recommend that you try one of our variations, below, or even come up with some of your own.

Once cooled, either keep them in the bread bin next to the crumpets to use in bread shortages, or see how we unlock its full potential in our Steak and Ale Pie with a Scone Dumpling Lid (see pages 100–1).

PESTO AND CHORIZO

The flavours in this recipe really pack a punch. We have a slight obsession with chorizo for its strong smoky and moreish taste. We have to hold back from trying to put in most recipes. When creating our savoury range this was our very first creation. We wanted a savoury scone that was miles away from your classic cheese number and got peoples' eyebrows raising. We looked to foods that we used all of the time and that were big on flavour and we came up with this bad boy … We think this one will put savoury scones back on the map!

FOR THE RADIO
'Around the World', Daft Punk

FOR THE BOWL
450g/3⅔ cups self-raising flour, plus extra for dusting
175g/1½ sticks butter
40g/2 tbsp + 1 tsp golden caster (superfine) sugar
2 large pinches of salt
2 large pinches of black pepper
100g/3½oz Spanish chorizo, skinned
1 tbsp smoked paprika
1 tsp garlic salt

FOR THE JUG
2 large eggs
4 tbsp buttermilk, plus extra for brushing
3 heaped tsp green pesto, plus extra for brushing
1 large garlic clove, crushed in a garlic press

FOR FLAIR
freshly grated Parmesan (optional), for sprinkling

Preheat the oven to 190°C/375°F/gas mark 5.

In a bowl, rub the flour and butter together gently through your fingers until the mixture resembles fine breadcrumbs or if you want to get the job done, give them a quick whizz in the food processor. Add the sugar, salt and pepper.

Next whip out the chorizo. Our tip is to finely chop, grate or blend it in a food processor – this works better than adding it in large chunks as it helps to distribute the flavour through the whole scone. Go for a ring of chorizo rather than slices as it packs more flavour. In a small bowl mix the smoked paprika into the chorizo (this helps to elevate the smokiness of the chorizo) and then add this to the mixing bowl with the dry ingredients along with 1 teaspoon of garlic salt. Mix thoroughly to combine. You will start to see the mixture taking on a red tinge.

In a jug, whisk together the eggs and buttermilk until light and airy. Add the pesto and garlic to this mix and whisk again to combine. Next the smell test. If you don't get bowled over by a garlicky pesto basil burst then sneak a bit more in the jug, but the 3 heaped teaspoons usually do the job. Make sure you use a good-quality pesto as the cheaper ones tend to not give it the same full flavour. Pour this mixture into the bowl and gently mix together with the dry ingredients.

Work the dough in the bowl with a wooden spoon or spatula until it starts to come together then finish with your fingers until the dough comes away clean from the edges of the bowl. Tip on to a lightly floured surface and work through with the base of your palm

3 or 4 times, each time folding the sides in and turning over until the dough becomes smooth. We love this bit as you start to see the paprika and chorizo spread into the dough.

Pat and shape the dough into a ball and roll out the dough until it is approximately 3cm/1¼ inches thick then, using a floured round cutter, cut out your scones. For posh nosh scones use the smooth side of the ring cutter and not the serrated side as this will give them a more professional finish.

Place your scones on a lightly floured baking tray, leaving enough space between each one for them to spread. Brush each one with buttermilk and dust with flour. Top each scone with a small dollop of pesto smoothed out over the top with the back of a spoon. For extra flair and wow factor add a small sprinkle of cheese – we recommend Parmesan – to give your scones a crisp golden top.

Bake on the middle shelf of the oven for 20–25 minutes, or until the tops are golden brown. To serve you can have it the All'Scone way, which is a nice helping of cream cheese and caramelised red onion chutney or our favourite: an old skool spread of butter and pâté to make it a mighty meaty bite.

FETA, GARLIC AND SPRING ONION

Living in East London means we have to serve up to many a discerning scone-eating palate. To keep up with the trendy foodie feeders we created this classy creation. Light, full of mouth-watering garlic and onion flavour with a creamy feta finish. This savoury scone will keep any tom, dick or harry happy.

FOR THE RADIO
'Electric Feel', MGMT

FOR THE BOWL
450g/3⅔ cups self-raising flour, plus extra for dusting
175g/1½ sticks butter
40g/2 tbsp + 1 tsp golden caster (superfine) sugar
2 large pinches of salt
2 large pinches of black pepper
1 tsp garlic salt
100g/3½oz feta cheese
3 spring onions (white and green parts), finely chopped

FOR THE JUG
2 large eggs
6 tbsp buttermilk
1 large or 2 small garlic cloves, crushed

FOR THE OVEN
1 egg, beaten

Preheat the oven to 190°C/375°F/gas mark 5.

Blend or mix in a bowl with your fingers the flour and butter until it resembles fine breadcrumbs. Add the sugar, salt and pepper, and garlic salt and then crumble in the feta. Add two-thirds of the chopped spring onions which includes all of the white part of the onion into the dry mix and set the remaining third which should be all green leaf aside for decorating later.

In a jug, whisk together the eggs and buttermilk until light and airy. Tip in the mashed garlic and give it a quick mix. Pour this mixture into the bowl and gently mix together with the dry ingredients.

Work the dough in the bowl with a wooden spoon or spatula until it starts to form together then finish with your fingers until it comes away clean from the edges of the bowl. Tip on to a lightly floured surface and work through with the base of your palm three or four times, each time folding the sides in and turning over until the dough becomes smooth.

Roll out the dough until it is approximately 3cm/1¼ inches thick then, using a floured round cutter, cut out your scones.

Place your scones on a lightly floured baking tray, leaving enough space between each one for them to spread. Brush each one with the beaten egg mixture to give them an amazing glossy golden finish and then, just before placing in the oven, sprinkle over the remaining chopped spring onion for decoration. Bake on the middle shelf of the oven for 20–25 minutes, or until the tops are golden brown.

These bad boys are great on a fresh spring day, served with cream cheese and spiced tomato chutney as a scone sandwich and being eaten whilst browsing round a trendy new foodie market.

WENSLEYDALE AND CRANBERRY

We found this combination after running a twitter campaign and asking our followers what they wanted to see in a scone. You can't argue with the classic combination of these two flavours. It's a staple on our cheese board after dinner and in a scone it creates a delicate creamy flavour that has become an unsung hero with our fans.

FOR THE RADIO
'A Kind of Magic', Queen

FOR THE BOWL
50g/½ cup whole cranberries, soaked (see method)
450g/3⅔ cups self-raising flour, plus extra for dusting
175g/1½ sticks butter
40g/2 tbsp + 1 tsp golden caster (superfine) sugar
2 large pinches of salt
2 large pinches of black pepper
150g/5½oz Wensleydale cheese

FOR THE JUG
2 large eggs
6 tbsp buttermilk

FOR THE OVEN
1 egg, beaten

Preheat the oven to 190°C/375°F/gas mark 5.

A little bit of preparation is needed for this one. To make sure your cranberries are extra plump and juicy and pop in your mouth when you're devouring them, it helps to soak them for a few hours before you're ready to start cooking. This helps rehydrate the fruit and stop it getting dry and shrivelled in the oven. Have some fun with this bit and try different things to soak them in. Keep it simple and just use water or get a bit more adventurous and use fresh orange juice or, our favourite, cherry.

Blend or mix the flour and butter in a bowl with your fingers until it resembles fine breadcrumbs. Add the sugar, salt and pepper. Crumble the Wensleydale into the bowl and mix in with the dry ingredients. Then fetch your pre-soaked cranberries, drain them and combine them with the rest of the mixture.

In a jug, whisk together the eggs and buttermilk until light and airy. Pour this mixture into the bowl and gently mix together with the dry ingredients.

Work the dough in the bowl with a wooden spoon or spatula until it starts to come together, then finish with your fingers until it comes away clean from the edges of the bowl. Tip on to a lightly floured surface and chaff 3 or 4 times until the dough is smooth.

Roll out the dough until it is approximately 3cm/1¼ inches thick then, using a floured round cutter, cut out your scones.

Not much decorating is needed for these ones, simply place your scones on a lightly floured baking tray, leaving enough space between each one for them to spread. Brush each one with the beaten egg mixture for a golden glossy finish. Bake on the middle shelf of the oven for 20–25 minutes, or until the tops are golden brown.

Serve warm with chutney and some sliced smoked Cheddar on top whilst sipping a glass of port next to a roaring winter fire.

HONEY AND MUSTARD PLOUGHMAN'S

We love a good picnic when the sun eventually begins to shine. This is a simple but tasty tweak to the basic savoury recipe and is the perfect replacement for crusty bread in a traditional ploughman's lunch.

FOR THE RADIO
'Hard Day's Night', The Beatles

FOR THE BOWL
450g/3⅔ cups self-raising flour
175g/1½ sticks butter
25g/⅛ cup golden caster (superfine) sugar
2 large pinches of salt
2 large pinches of black pepper
1 tbsp mustard powder

FOR THE JUG
2 large eggs
6 tbsp buttermilk
4 tsp wholegrain mustard
3 tsp clear honey, plus extra for brushing

Preheat the oven to 190°C/375°F/gas mark 5.

In a bowl, rub the flour and butter together gently through your fingers until the mixture resembles fine breadcrumbs. Add the sugar, salt, pepper and mustard powder. You can add more pepper and mustard powder if you want them to have more of a kick – we tend to be extremely generous with the pepper in these. You can also use a food processor for this if you don't have much time.

In a jug, whisk together the eggs, buttermilk, wholegrain mustard and honey until light and airy and fully blended. Pour this mixture into the large bowl.

Work the dough and wet mixture together in the bowl with a spatula until it starts to come together, then finish with your hands until it comes away clean from the edges of the bowl – you really do need to get stuck in! Once it has formed a large lump, place on to a lightly floured surface and chaff the dough a few times until it becomes super-smooth. Be careful not to get carried away and continue chaffing – it should be smooth after only a few times.

Roll out the dough until it is approximately 3cm/1¼ inches thick then cut out your scones, avoiding twisting the cutter – you want super-skyscraper scones and this will prevent this from happening.

Place your scones on a lightly floured baking tray, leaving enough space between each one for them to breathe in the oven. Bake on the middle shelf of the oven for 20–25 minutes, or until the tops are golden brown. Once baked remove from the oven and while still warm brush the tops lightly with honey, using a pastry brush.

Serve for lunch on a chopping board or in a lunchbox if you're on the run, with ploughman's classics such as cold meat, pickled onions, pork pie, cheese and chutneys.

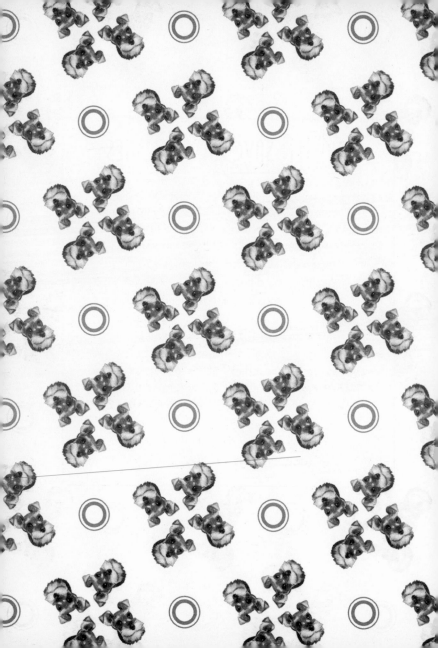

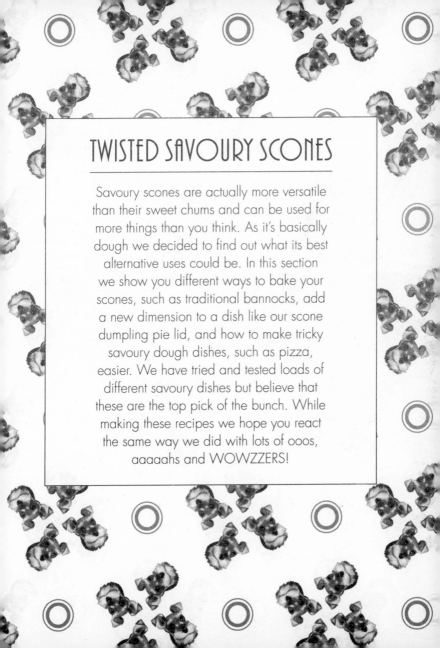

TWISTED SAVOURY SCONES

Savoury scones are actually more versatile than their sweet chums and can be used for more things than you think. As it's basically dough we decided to find out what its best alternative uses could be. In this section we show you different ways to bake your scones, such as traditional bannocks, add a new dimension to a dish like our scone dumpling pie lid, and how to make tricky savoury dough dishes, such as pizza, easier. We have tried and tested loads of different savoury dishes but believe that these are the top pick of the bunch. While making these recipes we hope you react the same way we did with lots of ooos, aaaaahs and WOWZZERS!

SUNDRIED TOMATO AND JALAPEÑO SWIRLS

We all like to show off a bit and these really add the wow factor to our table-top assortment and get the crowds forming. We eat them like plain scones but cut through them to show their swirly pattern through the middle.

Makes 10–12

FOR THE RADIO
'Heatwave', Martha Reeves and the Vandellas

FOR THE BOWL
350g/2¾ cups self-raising flour
100g/7 tbsp butter
a pinch of salt
4 tsp dried basil

FOR THE JUG
1 medium egg
10 tbsp buttermilk

FOR THE FILLING
50g/¼ cup jalapeños
50g/⅓ cup sundried tomatoes
4 tsp tomato purée
1 garlic clove, crushed

FOR THE OVEN
1 egg, beaten
a large pinch of flaked sea salt or rock salt
a large pinch of dried basil

Preheat the oven to 190°C/375°F/gas mark 5.

Blend together the flour, butter and salt until you have a fine breadcrumb texture, either with your hands or whacked in a blender. Add in the dried basil and mix through with your hands.

In the jug crack a medium egg and add in the buttermilk, whisk together and place to one side.

In a blender whizz together the jalapeños, sundried tomato, tomato purée and garlic to create a rough paste that will be the key to getting the spicy fiesta started. If you don't have a blender you can finely chop them and set to one side while you finish the dough.

Add the buttermilk mixture to the dry mixed ingredients. Cut through the mixture using a knife or spatula and form the scone dough, finishing off with your hands as it starts to come away from the sides of the bowl. Turn the mixture out on to a floured surface and chaff gently two or three times until the dough runs smooth (see pages 14–15 for chaffing techniques).

This dough needs to be rolled thinner than normal so that you can roll it up into a swirl. Roll it to a thickness of around 5mm/¼ inch, creating a large, flat piece of dough, around 17 x 24cm/7 x 9½ inches. To get perfectly formed swirls, make the edges razor sharp by cutting a neat rectangle from the dough with a sharp knife or, even better, a pizza cutter. Keep any offcuts to one side to be rolled out again.

Next, turn the dough so that the long end is facing you and slice the dough into 4cm-/1½ inch-wide strips; you should get around 6 from your first roll of dough. Avoid making them any wider than 4cm/1½ inches as the swirls will flop over in the oven – and who wants sad scones?

Take one of the dough strips and spoon 1–2 teaspoons of the tomato and jalapeño mixture on to the dough and spread it evenly over the strip with the back of the spoon stopping short at one end and leaving about 1–2cm/½–¾ inch of dough clear of the mixture. This bare part of the dough will be needed to stick the swirl together later. Take care not to rub your eyes with your jalepeño hand, like Grace did once… Drama. Now take the covered end and roll three-quarters of the strip up, then take the beaten egg wash and gently brush it on the bare end of the dough. Roll the rest of the strip up to the end. The egg wash will help stick the swirl together. Reshape the offcut scone dough and reroll and fill as before until you've used it all up.

Once all the swirls are rolled, line them up on a lightly floured baking tray like soldiers and finish with a sprinkle each of basil and flaked salt. Place in the oven on the middle shelf for 25 minutes.

Once baked, remove from the oven and allow to cool on a wire rack. The Mediterranean flavour of these works amazingly well with some hummus thickly spread on the top finished with a slice of tomato or cucumber of the top.

BLACK AND BLUE BANNOCK

A bannock is a traditional Scottish bread, and when cut into wedges these wedges are called scones. Our version is not strictly Scottish but deliciously rustic with a grown-up Stilton and blueberry twist.

Makes 8

FOR THE RADIO
'South Australia', Port Isaac's Fisherman's Friends

FOR THE BOWL
225g/1¾ cups + 1tbsp self-raising flour
1 tsp salt
1 tsp caster sugar
75g/5 tbsp butter
100g/3½oz Stilton
50g/¾ cup fresh blueberries

FOR THE JUG
1 egg
5 tbsp Greek yoghurt
3 tbsp milk

FOR THE OVEN
olive oil, for brushing

Preheat the oven to 190°C/375°F/gas mark 5.

Blend together the flour, salt, sugar and butter in the bowl using a blender or your fingers until you have a fine breadcrumb texture. Crumble in the Stilton with your fingers, then mix it into the dry mix, breaking down any large clumps.

In a jug, whisk together the egg, yoghurt and milk. Add the blueberries and the wet mixture to the dry and mix with the spatula.

The dough may appear a little dry to begin with but as you work the mixture together the blueberries will burst and begin to add moisture. This bit can get a bit sticky but the best way to bring this dough together is to get in there with your hands. Carry on until the dough forms one large lump.

Tip the dough out on to a lightly floured work surface. This dough will already have come together in the bowl and doesn't really need working, so you can just shape it straight away, although we like to give it a small chaff (see pages 14–15) just to get the blueberries bursting through the mixture which give it a more eye-catching look once baked. Simply round the dough by picking it up and do a tuck and turn twist to bring the sides under and help form a nicely round bottom (ooh er). It's a good idea to flour your hands as this stops the dough from sticking to them and helps round it easier. With a large knife score right through the bannock, dividing it into 8 scones. Brush with olive oil and bake on the middle shelf of the oven for 40 minutes. Maybe pull out your bagpipes for a spot of fine-tuning whilst you're waiting?

This posh loaf smells amazing when it's baking and will have people running to the kitchen. If it hasn't already been eaten before you get chance to serve it we recommend serving it warm or cold as an accompaniment to a cheese board and washed down with a nice glass of Rioja!

SMOKED CHEESE AND MARMITE
SCONE BITES WITH BEER

This was originally a large Marmite scone that we served on the markets but we decided to fuse the recipe with a Hungarian salt scone idea we were given from a friend. When made large it was a bit too much to handle so we shrank it and created these tangy, salty terrors.

Makes 10

FOR THE RADIO
'All Right Now', Free

FOR THE BOWL
225g/1¾ cups self-raising flour
3–4 large pinches of salt
75g/5 tbsp butter
2 tsp caster sugar
125g/1¼ cups grated smoked cheese
2 tsp mustard powder (optional)

FOR THE JUG
1 egg
4 tbsp buttermilk
2–3 tsp Marmite

FOR THE OVEN
3–4 tsp Marmite
smoked salt or sea salt flakes

FOR THE TOP
a sprinkling of dill

Preheat the oven to 190°C/375°F/gas mark 5.

Blend together the flour, salt, butter and sugar in the bowl, using a blender or your fingers, until you have a fine breadcrumb texture. Add half the smoked cheese to the bowl. Finally, if you have it, add 2 teaspoons of mustard powder for depth and warmth.

In the jug, whisk together the egg, buttermilk and 2–3 teaspoons of Marmite, depending on how serious your love for the stuff is.

Add the wet mixture to the dry and bring it together with a spatula and then your fingers. Roll out to 3cm/1¼ inches thick and, using a 4-cm/1½-inch cutter cut out bite-sized scones. You should get around 9 after re-working the dough.

Now for the messy bit. Transfer the scones to a lightly floured baking tray and get ready for decorating. To add that extra kick take a teaspoon of Marmite and push a small dollop (around a quarter of a teaspoon) on to the middle of each scone, using a skewer or cocktail stick. Then take the remaining half of the smoked cheese and place towering piles on each bite. Finally add a decent sprinkling of salt over the cheese. We recommend smoked salt but if you can't get that as it is a bit specialist then a good flaked salt will be fine. Bake for 15 minutes then transfer to a cooling rack until warm.

These are super-addictive with their salty cheesy taste and we guarantee you won't see them lying around for long. The best way to serve them in our opinion is with a sprinkling of dill. They are a great alternative to nuts or crisps as a drinking snack so their perfect companion is an ice-cold beer … and the football. Shhhh, don't tell Grace.

CHILLI BEEF S'CALZONE POCKETS

We love savoury finger food, but rather than just buying the usual snacks, we wanted to create our own. Stealing the idea of a calzone pizza and crossing it with a pasty (a firm favourite when we hit Cornwall in our campervan every summer), we created these, and called them …
S'Calzones!

Makes around 14

FOR THE RADIO
'Ring of Fire', Johnny Cash

FOR THE FRYING PAN
1 large onion, chopped
250g/9oz lean minced beef
1 tsp chilli powder
1 tsp chervil (if you don't have this try tarragon or parsley)
200g/7oz chopped tomatoes
150ml/⅔ cup hot beef stock
200g/7oz tinned kidney beans
1 tbsp tomato ketchup
olive oil, for frying
salt and pepper

FOR THE BOWL
225g/1¾ cups self-raising flour
225g/1¾ cups strong white flour
175g/1½ sticks butter
1 tsp salt
1–2 tsp chilli powder or chilli flakes (depending on how hot you are)

3 tsp black pepper
75g/¾ cup grated mature Cheddar

FOR THE JUG
2 large eggs
10 tbsp buttermilk
1 large garlic clove, crushed

FOR THE OVEN
1 egg, beaten
smoked paprika, for decorating

Preheat the oven to 190°C/375°F/gas mark 5.

Heat some oil in a large frying pan over a medium heat. Add the onion and cook until slightly softened, then add the beef. Cook until the meat has browned, then add the chilli powder, chervil and chopped tomatoes. Heat for a couple of minutes, then add the beef stock to the pan.

Wait for the stock to boil then reduce the heat and leave to simmer for 30–40 minutes. Ten minutes before the chilli is done, drain and rinse the kidney beans and add them to the pan along with the salt and pepper and our sneaky secret ingredient – a tablespoon of tomato ketchup. Trust us, this gives it the finishing touch! Simmer for another 10 minutes. Transfer to a bowl and set aside to cool completely. The mixture needs to be cold before it goes into the scone dough otherwise it will be too hot and will start to melt it.

In a large mixing bowl, rub together the flours and butter to form breadcrumbs. Season with the salt, chilli (HOT HOT) and black pepper, then add the Cheddar to the bowl and mix it all together.

In a jug, whisk the eggs, buttermilk and crushed garlic together until light and airy. Pour this mixture into the dry ingredients and gently combine, using a spatula.

Once the dough starts to form, take it out of the bowl and place it on a floured surface. Chaff the dough gently for a few minutes until it becomes smooth.

Cut the dough in half or into quarters and roll out the pieces until they are quite thin (approximately 5mm/¼ inch thick). Using a 10-cm/4-inch round cutter, cut out approximately 3–4 flat scones from each piece. Set the scone rounds to one side until you have cut all the rounds so you can fill them all at the same time. Repeat until you've used up all your dough, re-rolling the cuttings of dough as necessary. Once ready, spoon a teaspoon of the chilli mixture into the centre of each round and, using a pastry brush, lightly coat the edges of the dough with the beaten egg. Fold each one in half and gently press the edges together with your thumb to seal. To add extra detail once cooked dip a fork in some flour and crimp the edges of the s'calzones.

Place your s'calzones on a lightly floured baking tray and brush each one with the remainder of the egg. Bake in the oven for 30 minutes for a golden finish and crispy crust.

Once baked, give your s'calzones a final flourish by sprinkling with smoked paprika – this gives them an eye-catching fiery red glow. Serve warm or cold with a nice dollop of sour cream on the side.

STEAK AND ALE PIE
WITH A SCONE DUMPLING LID

This pie makes the perfect lunch or dinner on a blustery Sunday afternoon, served with heaps of veg. The twist is all in the lid! It is something we love to bake together when we have time to relax and make a gorgeous meal. You can use any ale or stout you like, but our favourite for this recipe is Guinness.

It's worth buying the best meat you can afford, and you can also add mushrooms if you like. Just take a good handful of chopped mushrooms (chestnut have a nice buttery taste) and throw them into the pan when you add your beef stock and ale. This will also fill out the pie more and make it last longer for leftovers or tomorrow's dinner with a hefty portion of chip-shop chips!

Serves 6

FOR THE RADIO
'Home', Michael Bublé

FOR THE PIE
1 onion, chopped
1 garlic clove, chopped
2 tbsp plain flour
500g/1lb 2oz braising steak, diced
300ml/1⅓ cups beef stock
300ml/1⅓ cups ale or stout
2 medium-sized potatoes
vegetable oil, for frying
salt and pepper

FOR THE LID
Simply follow the basic savoury scone recipe (see pages 72–3), adding 50g/½ cup grated Cheddar to the bowl ingredients if you want.
1 egg, beaten

Preheat the oven to 220°C/425°F/gas mark 7.

Add a drizzle of oil to a large frying pan over a medium heat. Fry the onion and garlic until golden and soft.

While the onions are frying, combine the flour with a pinch of salt and pepper then throw in the diced steak and coat the meat with the flour (this helps seal in the tasty juices while it's cooking).

Remove the onions from the pan and set them aside. Turn the heat up to high, add a little more oil and seal the meat in small batches, ensuring all the sides have been browned to seal in the tastiness. Too much meat in the pan at once will leave you with uneven coverage, so make sure your batches are small. Once all the meat is sealed, return it all to the pan along with the onions, beef stock and ale. Bring to the boil, then leave to simmer for 1 hour, stirring occasionally.

During this hour you can peel and chop your potatoes into bite-sized chunks. Place in a pan of salted water and bring to the boil. Simmer until soft, then drain. Alternatively you could be super energy-efficient and cook the potatoes in the same pan as the casserole as they'll absorb all those lovely beef flavours (it also saves on washing up). Just add the potatoes to the casserole dish after an hour with 150ml/⅔ cup water, and cook for another 15–20 minutes until tender.

Tip the stew into a large casserole dish, ideally a rectangular one. Leave to cool for at least 30 minutes, preferably next to an open window just like they do in the cartoons.

Now is the time to make your scone lid. Follow the basic recipe for the savoury dough on pages 72–3, adding the Cheddar to the dry ingredients, if you like. Once you have your scone dough, divide it into 6 equal pieces and shape into rough balls. These are going to make some scrummy scone dumplings for the lid.

Once your meat casserole is cool, bring the dish back to your work surface. This is the point to add a pie blackbird, if you have one. You don't need one for this recipe, but it still looks nice. We use ours as it reminds us of the pies our mothers used to make when we were children. Once the bird is in, take the balls of dough and line them in rows of three in the dish. Don't worry at this point if they are not touching, you'll soon see what happens when the pie comes out of the oven.

If you have any dough left over, now's the time to get creative! Roll it out and cut out anything that you want to adorn your pie with – we tend to go with leaves: simple yet effective! Place your adornments on your individual scone balls and brush the whole lid with the beaten egg.

Bake the whole thing in the oven for a good 25–30 minutes, or until the top is golden brown. When you take the pie out feel free to shout WOW as we did because the dough balls puff up to seal the pie, creating a gorgeous cobbled effect. Serve immediately with fresh steamed veg.

MONDAY NIGHT BUBBLE AND SQUEAK GRIDDLE SCONES

Griddle scones are actually the original scone. Scones started out in Scotland where they were cooked on a hot griddle over a fire. We decided to make these to use up leftovers from Sunday dinner when we had loads of mash and veg left. For this recipe we use cabbage but you don't need to be fussy with the veg; you can use anything you've got left in the fridge, really.

Makes 8

FOR THE RADIO
'Dreams', Fleetwood Mac

FOR THE FRYING PAN
1 red onion, diced
100g/1 cup cooked cabbage (or any other leftover veg)
a knob of butter
olive oil, for frying
salt and pepper

FOR THE BOWL
500g/1lb 2oz leftover mash or boiled potatoes, crushed
1 tsp Dijon or wholegrain mustard (optional)
350g/2¾ cups plain flour

FOR THE JUG
100ml/⅓ cup + 1 tbsp milk
2 eggs

Heat a drizzle of olive oil in a pan and fry the red onion for a couple of minutes. Next add the cabbage and season with salt, pepper and a knob of butter. Cook for around 3–4 minutes, then tip into a mixing bowl.

Add the potato to the bowl and mix it all together. Season again with a generous amount of salt and pepper; for an extra kick you can add a teaspoon of mustard at this point. Next sift the flour into the bowl and, using a spatula, mix everything together. Don't panic if you get a broken, bready mixture – this is what it is supposed to look like.

In a jug, whisk the milk and eggs, then add this to the dry mixture slowly, working with the spatula until the mixture starts to come together in a scone-like dough. Turn the dough out on to a lightly floured work surface and work it a couple of times with your hands until it becomes smooth. Round into a ball. You don't need to be tidy with these scones so pat the dough down into a large circle that is around 1cm/½ inch thick. Divide the dough into 8 triangles.

Now you're ready to griddle your scones. Heat some oil in the pan over a medium heat and fry 2 scone triangles for around 5–6 minutes on each side. Once browned remove from the pan and transfer to a warmed plate while you cook the rest of the scones in batches of two.

These scones work really well as an accompaniment to most meals with a bit of butter spread on them, especially with Monday night tea served alongside gammon and fried egg with a dollop of brown sauce.

EASY PEASY PIZZA

This recipe is great for finishing off bits and bobs from the fridge. Making pizza dough always seems a bit of a pain but by using scone dough as a base you don't need to worry about using ingredients like yeast.

The secret to a really tasty pizza is in creating a really tangy sauce with loads of flavour, but if you are stuck for time you could cheat and use pasta sauce from a jar (let's keep that a secret though). To give this one a nice rustic feel we used wholemeal flour to create the base and to try and show we are a little bit healthy some of the time.

Serves 4

FOR THE RADIO
'We Built This City', Starship

FOR THE TOPPING
2 large garlic cloves, chopped
1 x 400g/14oz tin plum tomatoes
4 tsp tomato purée
4 tsp dried oregano, plus a little extra to finish a dash of balsamic vinegar (optional)
leftover cheese and ham
1–2 tomatoes
olive oil, for frying and drizzling
salt

FOR THE BOWL
225g/1¾ cups wholemeal self-raising flour
a large pinch of salt
75g/5 tbsp butter

FOR THE JUG
2 eggs
3 tbsp milk

Preheat the oven to 220°C/425°F/gas mark 7.

Make the tangy sauce by heating a drizzle of olive oil in a saucepan over a medium heat. Add the chopped garlic and fry briefly to bring out the flavour. Open the tin of tomatoes and either chop them roughly on a plate to make sure you catch the juice or, if you feel messy, pour them into your hands and burst them into the pan through your fingers. Heat through to a rolling boil, then add the tomato purée. Season with a small sprinkle of salt and the oregano. If you like you can also add a dash of balsamic vinegar – we do!

Once the sauce has come to the boil take it off the heat and pour it through a sieve into a bowl to remove any lumps. Try to push through as much of the tomato as possible using the back of a spoon or spatula to force the lumps through. Once all the sauce is sieved place it back in the pan and bring it back to the boil. Simmer for about 10 minutes until it reduces down to a thick consistency.

Next, in a bowl mix together the flour, salt and butter to a fine breadcrumb texture with your fingers or in a food processor. In a jug whisk the eggs and milk together until frothy. Tip the contents of the jug into the flour mix and bring together to form a dough. Tip the dough on to a lightly floured surface and shape into a ball. To do this flour your hands and turn the dough, cupping your hands around it. Roll the ball out into a rough pizza-base shape that is no thicker than 5mm/½ inch. Because the dough is quite thin you need to be careful when moving it to the baking tray. A cheeky way of doing this is to roll the dough up over a rolling pin and then all you have to do is unroll it over the baking tray! Dust the baking tray with flour then transfer the pizza base to it and brush the surface lightly with olive oil.

Ladle or spoon as little or as much of the sauce as you like on to the base, typically this amount of mixture makes enough for 2 pizzas so we would go with half the mixture and save the rest for later in the week or to be frozen for another time. Spread it out evenly with the back of the spoon, covering as much of the base as you can and leaving a bare crust around the edge. Sprinkle liberally with ham and cheese and finish off with the tomato, a sprinkling of dried oregano (or basil) and a drizzle of olive oil. Bake for 15 minutes, until golden and the cheese has melted.

I'm sure we don't need to tell you what to do next but slice into triangles and serve with chips or salad! YESSSSS.

BASIL AND SALT SCONE DIP STICKS
WITH SOUP

We all love to dunk bread in our soup but scones taste amazing with soup too. However the round shape isn't always perfect for dunking so we came up with the idea of a scone stick. They're long and thin, a bit like bread sticks but a million times nicer – perfect for dipping in a cosy bowl of warm soup.

Makes 7–8 sticks

FOR THE RADIO
'September', Earth, Wind & Fire

FOR THE BOWL
450g/3⅔ cups self-raising flour
175g/1½ sticks butter
a large pinch of salt
2 large pinches of black pepper
a handful of basil, roughly chopped

FOR THE JUG
2 large eggs
8 tbsp buttermilk

FOR THE OVEN
1 egg, beaten
flaked or coarse sea salt
grated cheese (optional)

Preheat oven to 190°C/375°F/gas mark 5.

In a bowl, mix together the flour and butter until it resembles fine breadcrumbs. Add the salt and pepper. You can use your fingers or a blender. If you're using your fingers, finely chop the basil and stir it in at the end.

In a jug, whisk together the eggs and buttermilk until light and airy. Add to the bowl and gently mix with your friendly spatula, until it starts to come away from the bowl.

Lift the scone mixture on to a lightly floured work surface and divide it into 7–8 equal pieces. The best way to make your sticks is to roll them into long sausage shapes about 15–20cm/6–8 inches long. The trick is to roll the dough in only one direction. Our method is to place the dough under the palms of our hands and carefully pull our hands back over the dough and stretch it out. By sticking with only one direction for the roll you will get a much more even shape.

Once the sticks are rolled out place them on a lightly floured baking tray and brush them with the beaten egg. Finish them with a nice sprinkling of flaked or coarse salt and, if you feel extra naughty, a sprinkling of cheese.

Place on the middle shelf in the oven and bake for 20–25 minutes. Serve them with a nice bowl of soup, whilst watching your favourite TV programme.

RUSTIC CHEESE AND CHIVE SHARER

This little beauty is actually a top-selling flavour on our savoury list but we wanted to show you that good flavour combinations can be made into a tear-and-share loaf. We love munching on this after a long day and making plans while slurping lots of lovely tea made in the teapot.

Serves 8

FOR THE RADIO
'Your Song', Ewan McGregor

FOR THE BOWL
75g/5 tbsp butter, cut into chunks
225g/1¾ cups plain or strong white flour (or for an extra nutty flavour use half wholemeal flour), plus extra for dusting
1 tsp baking powder (baking soda)
25g/⅛ cup caster (superfine) sugar
a large pinch of salt
a large pinch of ground pepper
75g/¾ cup grated mature Cheddar plus a small handful for sprinkling

FOR THE JUG
1 large egg
75–100ml/⅓ cup–⅓ cup + 1 tbsp milk
a handful of fresh chives, chopped

FOR THE OVEN
milk, for brushing
black pepper, for sprinkling

Preheat the oven to 190°C/375°F/gas mark 5.

Place the butter in a large bowl. Add the flour and baking powder and rub the butter into the flour until it resembles breadcrumbs. You can also do this stage in a food processor. Next, throw in the sugar, salt, pepper and Cheddar. Mix well.

In a jug, whisk together the egg, milk and chives. Pour this mixture into the bowl and mix together with the dry ingredients using a spatula. Finish it off with your fingers and transfer the dough to a well-floured surface. Gently chaff the dough a couple of times to bring it together.

As this dough is quite sticky you can scrap the rolling pin and just use your hands and be extra rustic! Flour your hands and turn the dough as if you were using a potter's wheel to round it into a ball. Place the dough on a lightly floured baking tray, and pat it into a rounded, flat shape about 5cm/2 inches thick. Next score completely through the dough with your knife to mark out 4–6 scones and brush with a little milk. Sprinkle with a teensy bit of black pepper and some grated cheese and pop in the oven for 35 minutes, or until a knife inserted into the middle comes out clean.

Serve warm and tear into pieces to slather with generous amounts of butter and chutney, whilst wrapped up in a tartan blanket. A good brew of Assam goes down well with this sharer.

GOOD MORNING DROP SCONES WITH BACON, BANANA AND MAPLE SYRUP

This breakfast is the perfect excuse for getting everyone to sit around the table together early in the morning, so our advice is to serve everything together. To do this preheat the oven to a low gas mark; this will enable you to prepare all the drop scones and keep them warm while you finish off the rest of the accompaniments. In our opinion this is the best breakfast in the land and leaves everyone around the table with a HUGE smile!

Serves 4

FOR THE RADIO
'California Soul', Marlena Shaw

FOR THE BOWL
250g/2 cups self-raising flour
a large pinch of salt
50g/¼ cup golden caster (superfine) sugar
3 large eggs, beaten
200ml/¾ cup + 4tsp milk

FOR THE PAN
12 rashers smoked streaky bacon
a knob of butter and a dash of oil

FOR THE TABLE
2–3 bananas, chopped
maple syrup

Preheat the oven to 140°C/275°F/gas mark 1. In a bowl, sift the flour, salt and caster sugar and mix together with your fingers. Make a well in the middle and pour in the beaten eggs. Next put the milk in a jug and slowly start pouring it on top of the eggs, mixing with a wooden spoon as you do. It's best to get a bit of speed up on the mixing, if you're too slow you might get lots of lumpy bits so try and do it as fast as you can. Keep adding the milk until the ingredients form a thick batter that slowly runs of the spoon. This can also be done in the blender.

To cook the drop scones, heat a frying pan over a low to medium heat and add a knob of butter and a drizzle of oil. Next spoon in 3 dollops of the scone batter, one at a time, well spaced. Don't worry about the size and shape as each one will come out different, but allow the mixture to spread and settle before adding the next one so you know how much room you have in the pan to add each drop scone. Allow the scones to fry until the batter mixture begins to bubble on the surface. Using a spatula, flip each scone over and cook the other side. The batter will begin to rise and should have a golden brown colour to it. Once cooked, transfer to an ovenproof plate and keep warm in the oven while finishing off the remaining scones.

Once all the scones are cooked, clean out the pan and fry the bacon in a drizzle of oil until crispy.

Share the drop scones between your plates, stacking them on top of one other. For extra moreishness, melt some butter and, as you place each scone on the plate, liberally brush it with butter using a pastry brush. Place the bacon on top of the scone stack and then grab a handful of chopped banana and drop it over the bacon and drop scones. To finish, take the maple syrup and pour it over the top of the stack and watch as it slowly oozes its way down from the top of the stack to the bottom of the plate! GOOD MORNING!

SNACK CLUB

When Grace lived in Paris, inspired by the writer Gisèle Scanlon she and her friends formed a 'Snack Club'. They tried out new foods then scored their finds and compared notes. When we started dating we formed our own afternoon tea snack club, always with a large pot of a newly discovered tea as a palette cleanser. We want you to use this section for your own Snack Club notes on the recipes in this book. Which is your favourite? How did that first bite make you feel? Scores out of 10? Or have you added your own favourite flavours? How did it turn out? We'd love to hear all about your findings – post them on our website and who knows, maybe you'll see your flavour on our stall one day ...

ACKNOWLEDGEMENTS

We would like to take the time out to thank everybody who made this book possible.

Firstly, Caroline and the brilliant team at Square Peg for gluing it all together, and Jane for supporting us. Becka and her beautiful illustrations, of which we are so proud, and Emma, for looking after our baking mishaps.

Hackney Homemade for getting us started, and Kiersten at Victoria Yum, for always giving great advice and for being our inspiration. Eylem at Brew for Two, Louise at Brewodes and Dosa Deli, for your words of wisdom. Lorraine at Rosy Lee Tea, for superb insight and support, and for filling our bellies with your yummy tea and helping our stall look even better.

All of the Newick Towers pack – Jamie, Jo, Heather, Mark and Heidi – thank you for never growing tired (or at least not showing it) of our epic baking sessions.

Mom and Dad, Dom and Rory, Mum and Davvy, Span and Neil, Steph who is the best PA, Mike and also Lily, for giving great ideas for recipes; Aimz and Gem, Pam, Sabrina and Lauren and the rest of the dirty kestrels – so grateful to you all for being there when we needed you after baking disasters or just for a time out.

Adrian for his understanding and flexibility and the New Chapter crew for their enthusiasm, encouragement and tasting feedback, and Hannah and colleagues at F21 for your understanding and support.

Finally, Michael Bublé – for getting us through the darkest hours in the kitchen with your jovial Christmas songs, even if it was August.

INDEX